Dad and Mom gave me ice skates.
We will go to a place and skate.

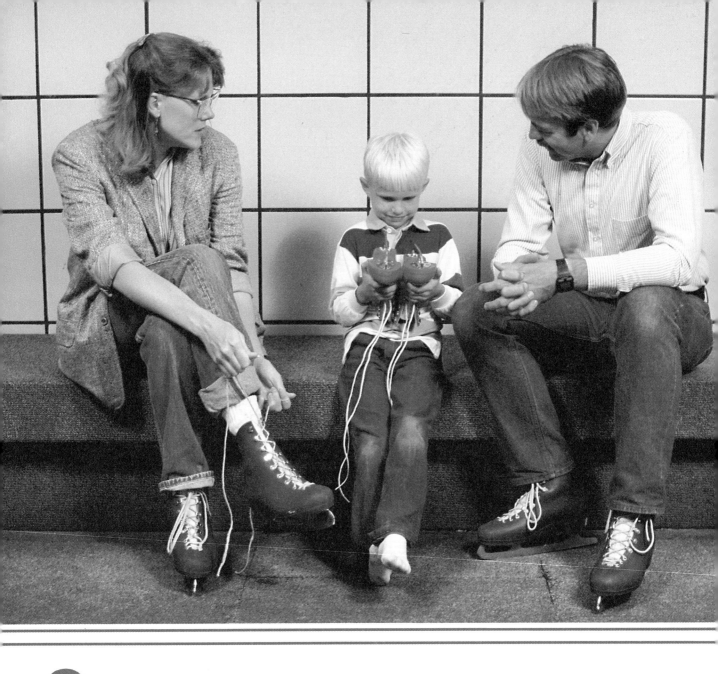

2

Do you see the two blades?
They will help me glide on the ice.

I am glad to be with Mom and Dad.
They will tell me how to skate.

3

4

Here we go!
I will skate close to Mom and Dad.
I do not want to slip and fall.

I go slow as I skate and glide.
Can you tell how far I slid?

5

6

I like to skate on the ice.
It is clear and flat like glass.

I will stay close to the wall.
It is a nice place to stop.

7

8

Oh no! Flip, flop, plop!
I am glad to sit for now!